THE GRATITUDE THEORY

The Ultimate Guide To Creating a Life You Truly Enjoy - One You Never Need To Escape From

July Cortes Cardenas

Copyright 2025 © July Cortes Cardenas.

All Rights Reserved.

No part of this publication may be reproduced, distributed, or transmitted in any form or by any means, including photocopying, recording, or other electronic or mechanical methods, without the prior written permission of the publisher, except in the case of brief quotations embodied in critical reviews and certain other non-commercial uses permitted by copyright law.

This publication is part of New Zealand's national collection, and it's publicly available at the National Library of New Zealand | Te Puna Mātauranga o Aotearoa.

ISBN (Paperback) : 978-0-473-76748-8

ISBN (HARDBACK) : 978-0-473-76750-1

ISBN (EPUB) : 978-0-473-76746-4

julycortescardenas@gmail.com

stan.store/julycortesofficial

New Zealand

It's not this book that will change your life; it's what you do with it that will produce the change in your life.

JULY CORTES CARDENAS

Contents

INTRODUCTION v

WHO DOES SHE THINK SHE IS? 1

MY FIRST ENCOUNTER WITH GRATITUDE 5

WHAT IS GRATITUDE? 13

GRATITUDE X FORGIVENESS 27

GRATITUDE X ACCEPTANCE 42

GRATITUDE X ENJOYMENT 57

GRATITUDE X ABUNDANCE 71

GRATITUDE X MANIFESTING 79

ABOUT THE AUTHOR 85

INTRODUCTION

Hands up if you think gratitude is saying "thank you" to the waitress, a polite manner or a Thanksgiving celebration once a year? It's often represented that way, but gratitude is far more than that. In fact, gratitude is kinda hard work, or at least it's a combo of consistent intention and effort that requires work if you want to play the long game. It's certainly that way if you want to achieve lasting results, such as joy, peace and abundance in a way that doesn't require you to reach for your wallet. Why? Because it flows from the ultimate source: yourself. That's the type of gratitude I'm talking about, and I'm going to show you in this book.

It's the gratitude that is not attached to an outcome, that is right here, right now and that speaks through constant attention and appreciation to the 'little things' given to you. It's the type of gratitude that acts as the foundation of inner joy, peace, love and abundance, so you can create a life you truly enjoy and from which you do not need to escape, or where you're waiting for an outcome to finally be happy.

So, where to start? Or what to do? 'The Gratitude Theory' will take you on the journey of understanding and embracing a gratitude mindset. Here is where it all begins: self-awareness, appreciating who you are and what you have, and enjoying it all. Forgiveness and acceptance are also part of the equation, as gratitude needs fertile soil to flourish. Nothing good grows on a barren heart.

This is a life's work, so don't expect it to nail it all at once, but understanding why gratitude is so important and how it can change your life, as it did mine, is a great place to start.

To live in a state of gratitude, you will need to prioritise the practices I mention in each chapter:

- Giving your attention and recognising what is present.

- Taking intentional action to express gratitude.

- Enjoying what you have.

- Being open to receiving gratitude from life.

After that, other practices help you stay in a state of gratitude, such as journals or gratitude prayers, minimising our forgetfulness and the habit of 'taking things for granted', especially when life gets busy. When applying the concepts in this book, you will be training yourself to be grateful for no reason at all. You will make gratitude your default natural state... and from there life flows effortlessly.

In gratitude, as in life, there is also space for feeling and expressing every emotion. Cry, scream, swear or spend your day alone. Don't deny those feelings or push them away; don't force yourself to feel positive if you don't feel like it, and don't rush your healing. Embrace your emotions completely without shame or guilt, and take all the time you need.

Gratitude is here and now, always available to you in the eternal present moment. It's in the small miracles of life – waking up, breathing, walking your dog, taking a tea, smiling, talking to your loved ones, or cooking a meal. When you add meaning and intention to your daily habits and routines, you practice gratitude, and it's in the compounding effect of practising them regularly that you will see life-changing results.

It's through the art of intentionally noticing the good in everything that I've trained my mind to see opportunities where I once saw only struggle and chaos, and most importantly, to trust myself when fear and self-doubt creep in. From this grateful state of being, I've rebuilt my self-esteem and manifested beautiful experiences, including trips, money, supportive people, and even international recognition. And while all of that is wonderful, my true achievement in life has been learning to live with a peaceful and joyful heart, no matter the obstacles, outcomes, or expectations of life.

In the end, is it not happiness that we are looking for anyway? After applying the practices shared in this book for many years and witnessing their incredible results, I can tell you with complete certainty: you already have everything you need to create the life you desire. Gratitude is your key to unlocking your full potential and reconnecting to your inner peace.

The Gratitude Theory is more than a book; it's a transformational resource that will lead you to the emergence of a joyful, peaceful and more abundant version of you. It's the emergence of the highest version of you who is available now in this very moment. Do not wait. Start here. Start now.

Chapter One

WHO DOES SHE THINK SHE IS?

Since my first memory, I've always felt that there was something different inside me...something that set me apart. I was the "crazy one," the exception. I had an insatiable curiosity to know, to explore, to learn, to see the world. I knew there was more to life than what I saw around me, and I wanted to experience it all. Even as a little girl, I refused to believe in the saying "born poor, die poor." No way. I knew I wasn't born for mediocrity.

That mindset became both my catalyst and my curse. On one hand, I longed to be accepted, loved, and have a normal childhood. On the other, I wanted to talk about success, travel, and becoming a millionaire. But in my environment, those topics were taboo and still are. Pursuing big dreams comes with a price: the courage to walk alone, to separate yourself from your environment, and to stay focused on your path. You cannot grow in the wrong soil. And if you find yourself in it, you must be willing to pull yourself out.

I had this mindset since I was five years old, but it wasn't easy. I wanted to fit in, yet I couldn't. The environment was harsh, and people could be cruel. My self-esteem took a beating early on. Still, my mother instilled powerful values in us: strength, hard work, independence, ambition and most importantly, honouring our name, our word, and our actions. She used to say, "Your name and what it stands for is your greatest asset."

I knew my journey would be long. But I also knew I wanted to walk it.

In my early twenties, I felt completely lost. Opportunities were so scarce that I couldn't see a way out. I studied cookery and pastry and not because I loved it, but because it was the only course available. I carried so much pain and resentment that I turned my anger toward God. But that didn't last long.

The further you move away from the light, the darker your path becomes.

I took every opportunity I could find as a stepping stone. My childhood dreams hadn't died; they'd grown bigger. Leaving my country became my obsession, my beautiful delusion. I took English classes, packed my bags in faith, and created a massive vision board that covered an entire wall in my room. I told everyone about my dream, even when they didn't believe me. I watched travel videos, visited agencies, attended seminars about studying abroad, and faced rejection after rejection. But I never gave up.

Studying abroad was incredibly expensive, so I started small businesses to increase my income. I worked relentlessly for nearly ten years without holidays, fueled only by that vision. I lost money, relationships, friends, and even family support, except for my mother, who believed in me unconditionally.

Then, in 2017, my dream finally came true. I became an international student in New Zealand, studying English abroad and starting a new life filled with hope and opportunity. It had taken me over 20 years to build this reality.

But It wasn't until I stepped outside my culture that I could finally see it all clearly. That's when my spiritual journey truly began. I had deep healing to do, people to forgive, traumas to process, fears and limiting beliefs to release.

That journey has been long, challenging, and humbling, but I chose to walk it. It opened my mind and heart, allowing me to see the lessons instead of the pain. I can now say with absolute certainty: I wouldn't change a single thing.

Looking back, I feel nothing but deep gratitude. Everything happened exactly as it was meant to. In truth, it was never about traveling the world or achieving big goals. It was about becoming the person I always meant to be. It was about the journey, not the destination.

It's when I look back that I can connect the dots. My past made me strong, kind, humble, resilient, consistent, hard worker… all those life skills that you must earn. It was genuine gratitude that helped me heal what I couldn't do with my conscious mind.

This book exists because the Universe asked me to write about gratitude, to share my life lessons and the secret practices that have guided me through my own journey. It's for those who are now walking a similar path, to help them find the strength, faith, and light they need to keep going, and also for those who have been looking for happiness in the wrong places.

May this book be your portal to a life you almost forgot was possible.

Chapter Two

MY FIRST ENCOUNTER WITH GRATITUDE

When I was 22 years old, I applied for a job as a kitchen assistant at a university. The selection process took an entire month, and when I finally started working, it turned out to be nothing like I had imagined. Three days later, I quit.

With the only paycheck I received from that job – a total of $30 – I decided to take a leap of faith and start my first small business: handmade chocolate truffles.

Of course, that money didn't last long. How could it? Before I knew it, I was already in debt. And when I ran out of options, when complaining, worrying, and overthinking did absolutely nothing, I finally did what most people only do when everything falls apart and there's nowhere else to turn…

(Drumroll please…)

I started praying.

And I don't know about yours, but my prayers used to be like this in those days:

"Please God, help me pay my debts, and please, please, please make my clients pay me this week, and my suppliers orders arrive on time tomorrow. Please God, give me more clients, so I can pay for my English course and travel the world, and I also need to buy a new computer, and don't forget to look after my family and the planet… and also God, I don't know what to do…"

I remember I heard a clear voice in my head saying:

"Why don't you say 'thank you' instead of asking so much. Don't you feel like a beggar?"

I stopped 'praying' immediately, and I felt embarrassed because it made absolute sense. I was praying from desperation instead of faith and trust. However, that divine message gave me so much clarity that the next day, I wrote a very special and unique gratitude prayer. But I'll admit, I did something a little naughty.

Since I still had debts to pay, I decided to do things differently: instead of begging or asking, I spoke my desires as if they were already done.

I didn't plead, I affirmed. I thanked the Universe as though everything I wanted had already manifested… and guess what? It worked.

That simple gratitude prayer became the only one I've ever truly needed. It has helped me in the good and the bad, even for manifesting the things that once seemed completely impossible.

Over time, I created a few variations of that same powerful prayer, depending on what I was calling into my life or the season I was in. And I want to share them with you.

Main Gratitude Prayer

"Thank you Father (or God) for everything I have, and everything I am.

"Thank you Father for looking after me, loving me and protecting me, and staying with me in every single moment of my life.

"Thank you Father! Thank you, thank you, thank you."

Note: This is the foundation, the place where we recognize our wholeness and remind ourselves that we are already loved, guided, and protected by God. We are never alone, and we never will be.

From this base, you can begin to build your own gratitude prayers by adding personal expressions of appreciation for what you wish to welcome into your reality.

For example, if you desire more money, start with the main prayer and then include the abundance and financial blessings that already exist in your life.

Here is an example:

"[Say main prayer first...] Thank you Father for all the money that I have in my wallet and bank account.

"Thank you Father for so much abundance, wealth, and prosperity I receive every single day.

"Thank you Father for my job and providing me with stability and safety. I feel so blessed, so loved and happy.

"Thank you, thank you, thank you."

Now, let's say you want something specific, then start with the main prayer and include a very detailed prayer of your dream.

Here is an example:

"[Say main prayer first..] Thank you Father because I'm working in my own business, I work from wherever I want and I love what I do. I'm earning 20x more than I'm earning now, and I'm serving my people, my community, my clients, and my audience to become the best version of themselves. I feel so free, so happy, and so fulfilled.

"Thank you Father for allowing me to share, to love, to give, to create and to change. For me, for them, for you, for nature, for the universe, for all of us.

"Thank you, thank you, thank you!"

Note: Every prayer must be spoken in the present tense, and it should begin and end with "thank you," as these words symbolize a wish already fulfilled. When we give thanks as if it is already done, we move from begging to declaring, from lack to faith.

Equally important is the intention behind your words. The energy you bring to your prayer is what gives it power. So don't just read or repeat the words, feel them. Let every sentence carry meaning, emotion, and conviction from your heart.

Here are some variations I have created using the same model I mentioned before:

Gratitude Prayer for Removing Toxic and Negative People Out of Your Life

"Thank you Father for everything I have, and everything I am.

"Thank you Father for looking after me, loving me and protecting me, and staying with me every single moment of my life.

"Thank you Father for removing that person (name it) out my life, for sending them away from me, far away from me.

"Thank you Father because that person is no longer close to me, and let them go with peace and love.

"Thank you Father! Thank you, Thank you, Thank you!"

Warning: This has truly worked for me, and here's what might happen: people may suddenly leave your life, they might resign, move away, change departments, or even countries. Or perhaps you will be the one guided to leave that person or that place. When something no longer serves your growth, God will remove you from it.

Prayers do work when you believe in them. However, prayer is not a shortcut to avoid inner work. You must also learn to set boundaries and truly know yourself, because you receive what you tolerate, and no one enters your life without your permission.

Yes, God protects you, but you still have to do your part. Faith is not passive; it's a partnership between you and life.

Gratitude Prayer for Protection When You Feel Unsafe or in Danger

"Thank you Father for everything I have, and everything I am.

"Thank you Father for looking after me, loving me and protecting me, and staying with me in every single moment of my life.

"Please, Father, push anyone away who wants to hurt me, make me invisible to all evil and danger, and bring me home absolutely safe. Please, Father, protect me with your divine mantle, so nobody can see me until I arrive home safe. Don't leave me alone. (Repeat this paragraph three times).

"Thank you Father! Thank you, thank you, thank you!"

Warning: I've said this prayer countless times, especially during moments when I felt unsafe, walking alone at night or taking the bus home. It truly works and has protected me many times.

However, I want to give you an important word of caution: use this prayer only when you genuinely feel physically unsafe or in danger. The purpose of this prayer is to make you "invisible" to anyone who may wish to harm you, and it's powerful. But if you repeat it too often, it can unintentionally make you "invisible" in other areas of your life as well: in business, in love, in social connections, or even when trying to be seen and heard on platforms like YouTube.

The truth is, no one can live a fully protected life. Even good people can hurt you sometimes, and your mind will always try to keep you safe, sometimes too safe. I learned this the hard way, so please, use this prayer with awareness and intention.

Quote

___

❝ Everything worth having demands your focus, your energy, and ❞ your devotion.

Chapter Three

WHAT IS GRATITUDE?

Gratitude is not just a word you say; it's a daily choice, a habit, a spiritual discipline, a state of being. It's the quiet trust in yourself, in God, in the universe, and in life itself — the trust that everything is unfolding for you, even when you can't yet see the full picture. It is the secret of all secrets and the foundation that shapes how we experience life.

Gratitude is not a fleeting emotion, a one-time act, a polite reaction, or an occasional practice you do only when things go well. It's not complacency or pretending to be content when you secretly desire more. It's not passivity, and it's definitely not mediocrity.

In the spiritual realm, gratitude is not about reacting; it's about creating. It takes conscious effort to focus on what is good, valuable, and meaningful in your life, even when life feels heavy, uncertain, or hard. Gratitude requires intentionality, and the same goes for happiness, joy, peace, love, success, and even health; they all require awareness and consistent practice.

Everything worth having demands your focus, your energy, and your devotion. That means happiness isn't "free." It's a sacred responsibility. You must protect it and not sacrifice it for the sake of other people's moods, opinions, or expectations. Your peace and your joy are not negotiable.

Life is what you focus on; therefore, if you consciously focus your attention on the right things in your life, instead of what's missing or not working, you start to unwire and rewire your brain, creating true transformation and evolution. That's how you become the creator of your world.

Life itself, the very breath within you, is the most precious gift of all. Be grateful for everything you are and everything you have:

- For your body and your health.
- For clean water, a safe place to rest, and the work that sustains you.
- For the people who share their time, kindness, and love with you.
- For your values, skills, and strengths—those gifts that make you who you are.

Don't overlook yourself:

- Are you responsible? That is awesome.
- Are you loving and kind? That is powerful.
- Are you fun, bringing laughter to others? That is a gift.

You already carry within you everything you need. The question is: will you be brave enough to use it? Every memory, every skill, every strength and even your fears, pain, and past mistakes can become powerful tools. They are not obstacles; they are your competitive advantage.

Everything you've lived through has given you wisdom. Those experiences can become a light to guide others facing similar challenges. Remember, you are unique. There is no one else like you, and no one can replace you.

Shift your perspective. Embrace the gifts, strengths, and resources you already possess. Gratitude is the key that transforms them into the building blocks of your ideal reality.

Misconceptions of Gratitude

Many misconceptions about gratitude prevent us from fully experiencing its power. Here are the most common ones:

1. Stigmas

Sometimes, expressing what we feel, being kind, loving, or grateful, can be misinterpreted. People might see it as being "too nice," flirting, or having hidden intentions, but genuine gratitude doesn't come from wanting something in return; it comes from the heart. It's not weakness, it's strength. It's consciousness. It's love in action.

2. Comparison

Another common misconception is comparing ourselves to those who have less or who are suffering more. If your sense of well-being depends on someone else's pain, that's not gratitude, that's ego. You're using another person's struggle to make yourself feel fortunate. Real gratitude doesn't need comparison; it recognises the blessing in what is, without judgment or hierarchy.

3. Assumptions

We often assume people know how we feel about them, that they know we love them, appreciate them, and are grateful for them. But if we don't express it, they might never know. Unexpressed gratitude is like a plant that's never watered; it eventually withers and dies. The same happens with our relationships, our health, and even our work.

We take things for granted because we assume everything is fine. We don't reach out, we don't say thank you, we don't express love until something goes wrong. We only connect when there's a problem, forgetting that life also happens in the quiet, ordinary, beautiful moments in between.

True gratitude lives in the everyday. It's not just for the highs or the lows, it's for the simple, sacred rhythm of life itself.

4. Complacency

A common misunderstanding is: "I'm grateful for what I have, so I don't need or want anything else." True gratitude doesn't mean settling. It means celebrating what is while staying open to what can be. You can be deeply grateful for your life and still desire growth, expansion, and improvement. That's the beauty of gratitude; it grounds you in appreciation while propelling you toward your highest potential.

Real gratitude says: "I'm thankful for what I have, and I'm excited for what's coming." That's not mediocrity. That's mastery.

Quote

❝ The so-called 'small things' are not small at all. They are the miracles that make your human experience possible. ❞

The Quadrant of Gratitude: "I AM"

The 'I AM' quadrant represents the inner world — your values, your skills, your strengths, and yes, even your weaknesses. It's the foundation of self-love and the root from which your entire outer world grows.

Yet, this is the area we tend to overlook the most. We're often grateful for what we have, but rarely for who we are.

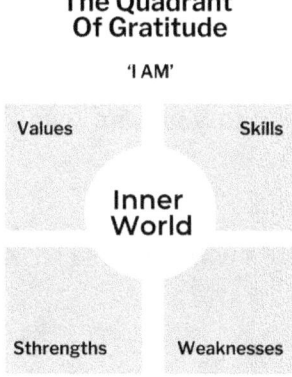

We don't usually say things like:

"I'm grateful for being kind."
"I'm grateful that I'm funny."
"I'm grateful that I'm patient, courageous, polite, or thoughtful."

We don't thank ourselves for knowing how to read, write, walk, or speak because we see these as "ordinary." We take them for granted, but the truth is, these so-called "small things" are not small at all. They are the miracles that make your human experience possible.

We think they're common and therefore not special, but the ordinary is where the extraordinary begins. Every great achievement starts with something small that someone chose to nurture.

If you know how to speak, and you give that ability a chance to grow, you might become a keynote speaker.

If you know how to write, and you give that gift time and effort, you might become an author.

If you know how to run, and you train with discipline, you might become an athlete.

The question is: Is it really small? Or have we simply stopped seeing its true potential?

When you have the courage and patience to keep cultivating yourself, to invest in your growth and believe in your own value, you begin to realise something profound:

You already have everything you need to create whatever you desire.

Your natural abilities, your learned skills, and your life experiences have been compounding quietly within you. You've been building value every single day, often without noticing it.

That's why awareness is so powerful. When you recognise and

appreciate your strengths, you unlock the potential to expand them.

So don't belittle them by saying, "Everyone can do that." No one can do it exactly the way you can.

Taking a photo doesn't make someone a photographer.

Running doesn't make someone an athlete.

Cooking a meal doesn't make someone a chef.

It's focus, practice, and belief that transform a natural skill into a gift, and that's where gratitude begins: in acknowledging the divine potential within you.

Create Your Quadrant of Gratitude
'I AM'

The first time I did this exercise happened almost by accident. I had to write my CV for university, and our tutor asked us to list our skills, everything we knew how to do. I took that instruction very literally and started writing every single skill I could think of, from walking to baking cookies to cleaning.

To my surprise, I filled more than ten pages with my skills, strengths, and achievements. Then I did the same with my values and even my weaknesses. I was honestly blown away. For the first time, I saw on paper how much I had already accomplished, and I felt deeply grateful and blessed.

This exercise is great if you want to change or start a new career or business and don't know where to start.

In fact, my business came directly from that list. And I invite you to do the same: take time to acknowledge your strengths, your growth, and your unique gifts. You might be amazed by what you discover.

Exercise

Write down all your skills, values, and strengths in detail, as if you were building your Life CV. Include everything you've learned from school, jobs, family, friends, community, and self-learning (books, social media, or online courses).

- Do you know how to bake? Write it down.

- Are you a great listener? Write it down.

- Can you read, write, organise, or teach? Write it down.

Once your list is complete, highlight the skills you truly love and excel at. Narrow it down to three that you can easily develop or improve. Then choose the one that aligns most with your values and has the greatest potential to impact your life.

Commit to it. Take massive action. Work on it daily. Consistency transforms potential into abundance.

The Quadrant of Gratitude: "I HAVE"

The *'I HAVE'* quadrant represents the outer world — the people, places, possessions, and experiences that surround us. This is what we usually see and acknowledge when we express gratitude. It's the visible reflection of our inner state because our outer world is shaped by our inner world.

Everything you have in your life right now is not random. It exists because of who you are.

The Quadrant Of Gratitude

'I HAVE'

People	Places
Outer World	
Possessions	Experiences

You got that job because of who you are.
You attracted that partner because of who you are.
You are consciously or unconsciously creating your own reality.

When someone chooses to hire you, to love you, to trust you, it's not just because of what you do or how you look — it's because of who you are inside: your values, your integrity, your kindness, your energy, your strength.

Clothes, titles, or appearances can change overnight, but your essence — who you are — is what truly builds and sustains everything around you. Your outer world is simply the mirror of your inner gratitude, reflecting back the energy you give to life.

Exercise: Create Your Quadrant of Gratitude 'I HAVE'

Write down at least one thing you are grateful for in each area of the quadrant: People, Places, Possessions and Experiences. They can be big or small, and then practice active gratitude. Here are some examples:

- Do you have someone in your life who is supporting you or has helped you in some way? Call that person and let him/her know.

- Do you have a shelter (home, flat, or even your car) that provides you with safety? Make some maintenance, cleaning or remove what no longer serves you.

- Do you have a job, side hustle, business or another type of income that provides you stability? Show up on time, keep growing, improving, and providing value to others.

- Are you in good health condition? Then go for a walk, dance, move your body or practice self-care. Having zero health issues is a luxury nobody talks about, until it becomes an issue.

Be grateful, but don't fall into the trap of becoming complacent or entitled.

Quote

❝ Don't let your pain keep writing your story; break the cycle. ❞

Chapter Four

GRATITUDE X FORGIVENESS

Forgiveness is setting yourself free from the energetic cords that keep you tied to the past. It's not about pretending the pain didn't happen, ignoring it, excusing it, or welcoming harmful people back into your life. Forgiveness isn't about them, it's about you.

It means choosing to stop carrying the heavy weight of resentment, anger, regret, shame, guilt, bitterness, and pain, burdens that slowly poison your mind, body, and spirit.

Unforgiveness is emotional clutter.
When you're holding on to the past, there's no room to receive anything new. It drains your energy and clouds your heart. The walls you build around yourself to avoid getting hurt again may feel like protection, but in reality, they trap you. You replay the pain over and over in your mind until it becomes your identity. You start copying and pasting the past into your present, and unknowingly, into your future.

Forgiveness is one of the most misunderstood forms of power. It begins with a choice, a decision that pain no longer gets to control you. Not because you've received closure or an apology, but because your peace matters more than holding onto suffering. Forgiveness isn't weakness; it's inner strength. When you release emotional clutter, your heart feels lighter, your mind becomes clearer, and you begin to breathe again.

Unresolved pain doesn't protect you; it erodes you. It changes the way you think, feel, speak, and connect with others. It isolates you, steals your peace, and leaves your body burdened with stress. Meanwhile, the person who hurt you may have long since moved on. They're free, but you're still carrying the weight as if the wound were fresh. That is the real tragedy.

Don't let your pain keep writing your story; break the cycle. Forgiveness is a full transformation of the mind, body, and soul. It soothes your nervous system, helps you trust again (especially in yourself), grounds you in the present moment, and connects you to something greater.

Here's how you begin:

1. Face the pain with courage.
   Allow yourself to acknowledge it. You're not just healing the past, you're choosing a new future.

2. Feel everything fully.
   Sit with the emotions, anger, sadness, shame, or guilt without judgment. This is where true healing begins.

3. Choose to forgive, not because they deserve it, but because you do. Sometimes, the person you most need to forgive is yourself: for abandoning your needs, people-pleasing, staying silent, or not standing up for yourself. Know this: you did the best you could with the knowledge, strength, resources and self-awareness you had at the time. You don't need punishment. You need compassion.

The Black Masters That Woke Me Up

I used to be a chronic people-pleaser, driven by fear. Whenever someone was unkind or intimidating, I would shrink to the size of an ant, completely paralyzed, afraid they might hurt me somehow. And because of that fear, many people took advantage of me.

I said "yes" to everything, even when I wanted to say "no." I ignored hurtful comments, tolerated disrespect, and pretended everything was fine, until the resentment and anger built up so much that I would eventually disappear, ghosting people because I was too scared to speak up.

That pattern led me into a painful cycle of guilt and self-blame. I started to see how often I had betrayed myself by ignoring my needs, overlooking red flags, dismissing my intuition, and allowing behaviors I should never have tolerated.

It took time to forgive myself for all the times I stayed silent, for choosing silence over self-respect. But through that process, I learned something priceless: how to set healthy boundaries, speak my truth, and walk away from people, places, and situations that no longer serve me.

I shifted my perspective and now, instead of holding resentment, I thank those experiences for waking me up. They were my Black Masters.

So choose forgiveness over resentment, guilt, or anger, and call your energy back. Let go of the old story, root yourself in the now, and once your heart is clear, gratitude will begin to bloom in its place.

When Forgiveness Doesn't Seem Like an Option...

I want to share this beautiful, but impactful story with you:

There was once a baby girl who was given away by her parents the day she was born. She was raised by her relatives, two aunties and an uncle who, unfortunately, gave her a life filled with pain.

From the age of five, she had to fetch water in a bucket for the household. Whenever something went wrong, or even for no reason at all, her aunties would hang her by her little hands, and naked, whip her again and again, like cattle. It was 1946, and women didn't have many rights and options. She never celebrated a birthday. She never received a Christmas gift or even a hug. She never went to school, nor was she ever loved, respected, or valued.

After years of suffering, one afternoon, she went for a walk and sat down in a trench. With her tiny hands resting on her cheeks, she said to herself:

"If God has given me life, I won't allow these people to take it away from me."

That day, carrying nothing but her will to live and an incredible love for life, she walked away and never went back. She was only seven years old.

She found shelter in different homes, working as a domestic cleaner, moving from house to house and city to city, doing whatever she could to survive. Having never known a real family, she dreamed of building her own one day, of going to university and giving her mother, whom she had never met, a better life.

Years later, when she was aged 20 and close to giving up on life, she met a kind man. Despite her fear and the risk of trusting again, they chose to build a life together. From their union, a family was born, and nine children came into the world. I am the youngest.

Life was far from easy. My older siblings suffered too, growing up with a mother who carried deep trauma and pain. Yet my parents worked tirelessly to give us the little they could, even while living in extreme poverty. My father eventually found a job as a cook in a hotel, while my mother continued cleaning houses and caring for all of my siblings.

When my siblings became teenagers, my mother started dreaming of owning a home, a place that was truly ours. One day, while she was on the bus, she overheard people talking about land for sale in the south of the city. When she got home, she told my father. The deposit was only $100, and, thanks to the habit of saving she had taught my siblings, they had exactly that amount.

As for the rest of the payment, my father had been working for years and had accumulated savings and holiday pay, which could only be used for buying a house or retirement. The amount matched perfectly. With that, they bought the land, and for the first time, our family had a place to call home, breaking the first layer of extreme poverty. By the way, I was born in that house.

From there, a new story began. My siblings went to public schools, and my parents made it clear: "We can only give you high school; the rest is up to you."

And so we fought. We studied. We worked hard. Every small victory was paid for with sweat and tears. But with each win, we broke the cycle a little more, climbing higher and higher.

Today, my siblings are entrepreneurs, teachers, and engineers, hardworking, kind and talented people. My mother has travelled abroad many times and now lives peacefully in the home she built with her own hands. My father passed away many years ago at 57, but his legacy lives on in each of us.

There is still one missing piece in this story, though...

Remember when I said my mother never went to school? That was the only thing she couldn't forgive her relatives for. Her dream was to go to university and become a teacher – a dream that never came true. It remains an open wound, a quiet grief for the life she never had. Her gratitude to God and her love for life carried her far, but that scar will never fully heal.

Every time she comes back to the memories of the past, I bring her back to the present moment, and I remind her of all the great things she has accomplished, and I fill her heart with gratitude, peace and success.

I often tell her this:

"Mom, maybe you never had the chance to study or become a teacher, but you did the best you could with what you had. You achieved the impossible. You broke chains that could have crushed anyone else's soul. Our success is your success. My success is your success. Without you, none of us would be where we are today. You truly made it."

If I could, I would give my life to make her dream come true. But since that's not possible, I'll dedicate my life to making hers as beautiful and joyful as I can.

And for you, if she could, so you can.

The Dark Masters

I call the "Dark Masters" all the people, experiences, and situations that hurt me, broke me, judged me, and forced me to grow. They were not gentle teachers. They didn't arrive with kindness, but with pain, and yet, they pushed me to level up, to set boundaries, to speak my truth, to love myself, though not in the loving way it could have been.

For years, I lived in the past, haunted by the faces, words, and circumstances I wanted desperately to forget but couldn't. I tried to forgive and let go through meditation, journaling, and even hypnosis, but something was missing. I hadn't yet understood the purpose these people and events held in my life. Why did they come? Why did they treat me so poorly? Why did it feel like they hated me?

That teacher in primary school who told me that I was never going to do anything in my life. Who say that to a six-year-old child?

Or as an adult, having to deal with so many betrayals and abandonment, toxic and judgemental friendships, jealous relatives, and arrogant bosses and co-workers.

According to the Law of Vibration, we attract experiences that match our frequency. At first, it was painful to admit that I had attracted those dark seasons and the people who mirrored my wounds, but then came a deeper realisation: perhaps they weren't curses, but catalysts.

Looking back, I see the truth. If those obstacles had never shown up, my life might have been easier, but it also would have been average, predictable, and small. I would never have left my home country. I would never have learned English, which opened doors to knowledge and opportunities unavailable to me before. I would never have travelled to the other side of the world—a journey that transformed everything. I would never have stretched, broken, and rebuilt myself into the person I am today.

Never fitting in turned out to be one of the greatest gifts God gave me. It took years of struggle to see it, but I now know that nothing extraordinary is born from comfort. True joy and growth live outside it. People with great potential are not meant to settle. They are not meant to move with the herd.

Those who blamed, betrayed, abandoned, humiliated, or pulled me down were not destroying me; they were dismantling the false identities I had outgrown. Piece by piece, they stripped away the parts of me that didn't belong to the highest version of myself. They thought they were breaking me, but in truth, they were shaping me, and now, when I look back at how far I've come, I can honestly say: I thank them.

The Dark Masters are here to test our values, our boundaries, our self-worth, and our awareness. They show us what still needs to heal and what we must release.

Just like a car goes through rigorous testing to reveal what needs repair, the dark masters reveal the blind spots in our spirit, and they are not always people. Sometimes they appear as illness, loss, accidents, or financial collapse; anything that forces us to shed the old, to wake up, to rise higher.

The dark masters are not here to punish you. They are here to prepare you.

The Light Masters

Once the Dark Masters have broken you and cracked your ego, challenged your worth, and pushed you to evolve, the Light Masters arrive. Their work can only begin after you've made space for transformation.

The Light Masters are like the 'angels on Earth', the people, situations, and even objects that illuminate your path and restore your belief in what's possible. They bring you clarity, love, wisdom, support, new opportunities, abundance, peace, and joy. They've always been around, but when you're consumed by fear, negativity, or stuck in old patterns, you simply can't see them. You miss the signs, even when they're right in front of you, because you're still operating from your old identity.

Light Masters can only guide and uplift you if you allow them to. When they appear, it's up to you to recognise and receive their presence. If you unconsciously reject their support—through fear, mistrust, or self-sabotage, they will eventually leave... or be taken from you, and in their place, a Dark Master will return until the lesson is finally learned.

Light Masters as People

They can come in many forms:
A parent, a teacher, a mentor, a partner, a friend, a kind stranger.

What defines a Light Master is not who they are, but the impact they have on your life. They show up at pivotal moments, often when you're in the transition phase, and offer just what you need to take your next step.

Examples of Light Masters in human form:

- A loving partner who supports your dreams while you find your wings.

- A friend who believed in your vision and lent you the money to start your business.

- A mentor or teacher who saw your potential before anyone else did.

- A stranger who saved you from danger or offered a word that changed your perspective and life.

- A boss who trained you with highly valuable skills that led to your breakthrough.

The Right Guide Appears When Needed

Famed artist **Devon Rodriguez** was once rejected from the High School of Art & Design because his skills weren't developed enough. Instead, he attended Samuel Gompers High School in the South Bronx, where he met an art teacher who believed in him, helped him build his portfolio, and mentored him. Thanks to that Light Master, Devon reapplied, was accepted, and today, he is one of the most followed and celebrated artists in the world. (Source: Official Instagram @devonrodriguez).

Light Masters as Objects

Sometimes, Light Masters aren't people at all, but meaningful objects that supported you through entire chapters of your life, or as the outcome of your biggest dream in life. They may seem ordinary to others, but to you, they represent resilience, devotion, and success.

- A cheap car that was your home, never let you down and got you where you needed to go, or the dream car you thought you would never have, until one day, you got it.

- A worn-out backpack that carried you through university, jobs, travel, or business.

- A piece of jewellery, such as a ring, a watch, or a bracelet, that was with you on major milestones: your first big trip, or the launch of your business.

The Red Backpack That Carried a Dream

Entrepreneur **Sara Blakely**, founder of Spanx, held onto a red backpack she wore every day while building her business. Today, it's a powerful symbol of her journey, reminding her of the grit, sacrifices, and miracles along the way. (source: Official Instagram @sarablakely).

Light Masters as Moments

Sometimes, the Light Master is a moment, a divine alignment or a sudden breakthrough. These are experiences of synchronicity, serendipity, or divine timing, when you are exactly where you need to be, even if it doesn't make sense at the time.

These moments change the direction of your life. They affirm that you are loved, supported, and guided by something greater than yourself.

When I arrived in New Zealand for the first time in 2017, something miraculous happened. I was unexpectedly upgraded from economy to first class free of charge. I hadn't requested it. I hadn't done anything special. The flight attendant simply said, "Your offer was accepted. You've been upgraded to first class." For someone who came from poverty, that moment was unforgettable. I still carry that memory as a reminder that anything is possible.

You Can Be a Light Master

You become a Light Master every time you give from a place of service, without judgment, conditions, expectations, or codependency. When you uplift others simply because you can, you're not just helping, you're shifting destinies, healing generational wounds, and creating ripples of change across the world. To give unconditionally is one of the most powerful forces in existence. It is a divine act of service.

Remember:

Dark Masters awaken you.

But Light Masters rebuild you.

Quote

❝ The life you live now is full of answered prayers, don't let forgetfulness turn blessings into burdens. ❞

Chapter Five

GRATITUDE X ACCEPTANCE

It's easy to feel grateful when life is going well, when our prayers are answered, and when things unfold as we hoped, but real growth begins when we can practice gratitude even in the middle of chaos. It's recognising that life itself is a gift, and every gift comes with challenges meant to help us grow. Truthfully, we don't grow in the easy times; we grow in the hard ones.

Acceptance is not giving up.

It's not pretending everything is perfect or forcing "toxic positivity." Acceptance is simply choosing to stop controlling and resisting what is. It means meeting yourself and your circumstances exactly where they are without judgment. When you resist, complain, or hate something, you give your energy away. You become entangled with what you don't want, and that very resistance feeds it, making it stronger. Therefore…

- If you want a new relationship, stop hating being single.

- If you want a dream job, stop resenting your current one.

- If you want to transform your body, stop waging war against it.

What you resist, persists. Make peace with where you are.

Instead, shift step by step:

- From resistance → to acceptance.
- From acceptance → to neutrality.
- From neutrality → to gratitude.

Gratitude dissolves resistance. It removes the energy you've been pouring into negativity and redirects it toward peace, clarity, and possibility. That's when life begins to move again.

Remember: your current situation is temporary. Something better is already on its way. By softening your energy, dropping resistance, and making peace with the present, you open the door to new opportunities and blessings.

Almost everything you have now was once something you prayed for. That job you complain about? You applied for that opportunity. The partner you now take for granted? You once prayed for their arrival when you were single. The life you live now is full of answered prayers, don't let forgetfulness turn blessings into burdens.

With every new level comes new challenges, and they are invitations to expand, not punishments to endure. Don't become a victim of life, your circumstances, or what has happened to you.

What Can You Really Control in Life?

Yourself:

1. Your beliefs.

2. Your thoughts.

3. Your opinions.

4. Your desires (what you want and don't want).

5. Your actions.

So, if you struggle to control even yourself, how can you expect to control everything else?

How I Healed My Toxic Relationship With Acceptance

If there was one word that used to make me sick, it was acceptance.

That word doesn't come easily when you're at your lowest, when nothing makes sense, when you've done nothing wrong, yet it feels like life is punishing you simply for existing.

It took me years to understand what "acceptance" truly meant, and even longer to live it. It wasn't a single moment of enlightenment or a one-off decision, it was a slow unfolding. A series of small actions, micro-wins that quietly accumulated over time until they reshaped my entire identity.

Little by little, I rewired my brain to accept every part of myself, the bright and the broken, the confident and the ashamed, to own what I truly desired in life without guilt or apology, and to release what no longer resonated with who I was becoming.

One of my greatest lessons in acceptance came through my struggle with self-esteem. I was born with big dreams and an enormous vision of myself. When I was only seven years old, I would talk about travelling the world, learning new languages, and being wealthy. I even had a game I played for hours, pretending to call my "employees" on an imaginary phone:

"Please, buy me that house I saw in the magazine, the one with two rooms and close to the beach. Thank you." Click.

"Book me that trip to Paris for this weekend. Thank you." Click.

I could go on for hours. I wasn't bored for a second. My imagination was my playground, a portal to a reality that felt more real than the one around me.

But in the eyes of others, I was delusional.
And when you're freaking poor, dreaming big isn't considered brave, it's considered stupid.

I quickly realized that my mother and I were the only ones in our world who dared to dream big. That made the journey a bit lonely. To this day, I can count on one hand the number of people I've met who truly want to do something meaningful with their lives.

As a child, that realization was confusing and painful. I couldn't understand why having dreams was something to be ashamed of. I felt like I didn't belong anywhere. I often imagined moving to another country and seeing more of the world because deep inside, I knew I was meant for something more.

Over time, I struggled to connect with anyone, except my mother, and I began to hate myself for not being "normal." I was labeled ugly and unintelligent, even bullied by my teachers. I remember thinking:

"What's the point of talking if no one listens or understands me anyway? It's better to stay quiet."

So I stopped talking. I withdrew into silence, even when surrounded by people. My self-esteem hit rock bottom. My inner dialogue became brutal. I convinced myself that something was wrong with me. That it was all my fault. That nobody loved me. That I didn't even deserve to exist. I couldn't bear to look at pictures or videos of myself.

Everything changed the day I finally left the country where I was born, just as I had promised myself at seven. It was only then that I truly began to heal. One random day, I made a conscious decision:

"I will love and accept myself, no matter what."

I was tired of the constant self-abuse inside my own mind. That moment marked the beginning of my spiritual awakening.

I went all in. I allowed myself to grieve, to feel, to embrace every drop of sadness, guilt, shame, and resentment I had buried for years. I faced the unspoken words, the broken promises, the people-pleasing disguised as kindness, the emotional abuse disguised as "culture."

The steps were simple, but powerful. Every night before bed, I whispered a single affirmation:

"I am happy."

I repeated it again and again, with the pure intention to reprogram my subconscious mind. I did it religiously, until something clicked inside me. Then I added new affirmations:

"I am beautiful."
"I am smart."
"I am rich."

Soon after, I began meditating and practicing hypnosis. With every small win, the voice in my head transformed, from my harshest critic into my biggest coach and cheerleader.

That was my first real victory in life, and to me, it means more than anything else I've achieved.

Then I took on the harder ones: shame, guilt, people-pleasing, fear of judgment, fear of speaking up. That part was wild because it required action. Affirmations alone weren't enough. It took daily, consistent effort, and an unwavering desire to change. Slowly but surely, I rebuilt myself from scratch, releasing what no longer served me and reawakening my wild, dreamy inner child who believed she could have it all.

After reflecting deeply, I realized there are two types of events that shape our lives:

1. One Time Events

These are the unpredictable storms, accidents, serious illness, tragedies, bankruptcy, natural disasters, or even sudden blessings like winning the lottery. They come without warning and change everything. No matter how strong, spiritual, or successful you are, these moments will bring you to your knees.

Here, acceptance doesn't come naturally, and honestly, it shouldn't. You have to grieve. You have to feel. Don't rush to be "positive." Don't force yourself to act like everything's fine when it's not. Feel your pain fully, let it move through you, find support, and when it's time to move on, you'll know.

2. Regular Events

These are the everyday experiences that quietly define who we become, how we talk to ourselves, what we eat, what we read, what we believe, how we spend our time. They are shaped by our upbringing, culture, and environment. Here, acceptance is a choice. Sometimes it takes a second; sometimes it takes a lifetime. But once you choose it, your life begins to flow differently.

I only found joy when I trained myself to be joyful for no reason at all. Gratitude and joy became my natural state, even when life feels tough I remind myself this statement:

"I'm not going to make my life a misery, no matter what. I will find a way or I will create one."

And that is what true acceptance feels like to me.

The Trap Of Complaining

"A complaining mind is never peaceful, never happy, never grateful — and nothing is ever enough for it."

Complaining feels rewarding in the moment; it can bring attention, affection, or approval, but it steals your peace. A complaining mind is never calm, never grateful, never truly happy, and no matter what happens, it always finds a reason to complain. If you complain about what you already have, why would you be entrusted with more? Complaining comes naturally when we don't like something, multiplying problems, but gratitude has to be intentional.

Complaining invites negativity and drama, while gratitude rewires your brain to notice miracles. That's why it's powerful. Every time you feel the urge to complain, pause, shift into acceptance, and then deliberately look for something even small to be grateful for.

Your life already holds more meaning than you realise. If you woke up today and none of your loved ones died, you've already won. Life is made of 'small miracles', and when you honour them, they grow into something greater.

The Power of Your Words

Your words shape your reality. Every word you speak is a command to your subconscious mind. Black humour, sarcasm, complaints, or affirmations, it doesn't matter whether you "mean" them or not; your brain records them as truth. Words are vehicles, and every word sets a direction. So choose carefully. Speak healing, speak hope, speak gratitude.

Exercise: Practice Intentional Gratitude

Use two simple but powerful words "thank you." Walk around your home or workplace and say it aloud to everything you see:

- Clean water? "Thank you."

- Food in your fridge? "Thank you."

- Money in your wallet—even one dollar? "Thank you."

The gift of waking up this morning? "Thank you."

Replace complaints with gratitude. Use your words not to destroy, but to create, heal, and manifest. Gratitude shifts your entire state of being, and from that place, life transforms.

Quote

❝ If you want a change in your life, then make it. Otherwise, nothing changes. ❞

The Power of Neutrality

Neutrality is the ability to step back and stop labelling a situation as good or bad, positive or negative. It's not about forcing yourself to be positive or pretending everything is fine. Instead, it's about no longer pouring your attention and energy into what you don't want, and it's no longer giving your energy or attention to something (or someone) that doesn't want you, or serve you.

Neutrality is finding peace in the present moment, opening yourself to new opportunities and reclaiming the power you once gave away.

This was one of the best practices I ever did while transforming my cruel inner voice. Trying to be happy felt impossible, especially when my mind was on fire and my heart was heavy. But everything changed the moment I realized I didn't have to force happiness.

Instead, I allowed myself to simply be neutral. I didn't have to be happy, but I also didn't have to be sad. From that space of calm neutrality, where I stopped fighting with my mind and emotions, I finally found relief, and in that quiet pause, I could intentionally choose gratitude and joy over sadness.

This state is not permanent, though; it's temporary, a pause, but it's a powerful place to be, because it's where you can make your best decisions.

How to Shift into Neutral State

When emotions are high, clarity is low. Neutrality gives you the space to see things as they truly are, not as your fears or frustrations make them seem.

To shift into this space, engage in activities that ground you and bring you back to the present moment:

- Take a break, it could be an hour, a day, or even a week.
- Go for a walk in nature, or take a short trip to clear your mind.
- Move your body, dance, run, stretch, practice yoga, work out or practice a hobby you enjoy.
- Talk to someone who uplifts you, a coach, mentor, therapist, trusted friend, or spiritual guide.
- Journal your thoughts or meditate to release the emotional charge.

Remember: You don't need to give up, you just need to pause. Step back, breathe, calm your body and mind, and then return. What's important is that you come back with clarity.

Why Neutrality Matters

When you make decisions from frustration, sadness, or fear, they are often decisions you later regret because they're driven by desperation, not peace. Neutrality helps you calm your mind, balance your emotions, and reset your energy. From this space, you can choose differently, for example:

- If someone betrayed you, choose forgiveness.

- If you hate your job, start looking for a new one.

- If you want more meaning in life, help others.

The Call to Change

If you want a change in your life, you must choose it. Otherwise, nothing changes. Too often, people go back to what's familiar even if it makes them feel unfulfilled: the old job, the ex, the patterns that keep them stuck.

Use this pause to design the life that you truly want, and intentionally take aligned action, and move forward in the direction of your ideal reality every single day.

Quote

❝ The proof that you are living a fulfilling life is not in what you have, it's in the joy that you are manifesting from within. ❞

Chapter Six

GRATITUDE X ENJOYMENT

Gratitude roots you in awareness, while enjoyment allows you to express that awareness through action. Every present moment carries an opportunity, a blessing, an experience, a simple gift waiting to be acknowledged.

There are two definitions of enjoyment.

The first is short-term enjoyment: The pleasure, satisfaction, or happiness we feel when we experience something, like listening to music, watching a movie, or eating our favourite food. It's about enjoying the moment.

The second is long-term enjoyment: The fulfilment that comes from doing something, like learning to play an instrument, writing a book, or building a business. It's not just about the moment, it's about growth, mastery, and purpose over time.

The real difference?

I can listen to music every day of my life and feel good for a few minutes, but that alone won't make me a musician or change my life. However, if I play an instrument, in ten years I could develop a new career, a new identity, and a new level of mastery.

Both are beautiful and necessary. There's nothing wrong with short-term enjoyment. Going to a concert, eating at a nice restaurant, or relaxing at home, these moments nourish the soul, but there are also areas where we naturally invest more energy, passion, and time. Those become long-term projects and paths that shape who we become.

Enjoyment vs. Instant Gratification

The difference between enjoyment and instant gratification lies in the intention behind it.

If you're listening to music to avoid your emotions, to escape sadness, anxiety, or boredom, that's not enjoyment; that might be procrastination, a trauma response or a coping mechanism. It's a way to cover up fear or discomfort rather than connect with joy or yourself.

True enjoyment is intentional, conscious and present with what is, until it becomes your natural state, when you feel joyful for no reason at all. It's not about chasing pleasure, avoiding pain, feeling constant happiness or forcing positive emotions.

How to Start Cultivating Enjoyment

My daily routine is filled with tiny practices that add joy during my day. These are my favourites:

Be grateful for the breath in your lungs and then enjoy it. Take a deep breath and feel the air entering and leaving your body. Notice the fresh air as it flows through your nose, your lungs filling, your chest expanding. Feel the release as the breath leaves, and observe how your body relaxes, how your mind calms. This is the gift of being alive, something to be felt with every cell of your being.

Throughout your day, pause. Set aside distractions and, even for 30 seconds, truly enjoy your life: the sunlight streaming through your window, the rhythm of the rain, the aroma of coffee or tea, the warmth of your own heartbeat. Each of these moments is sacred.

Don't fall into the trap of believing today is "just another day." It isn't. Today is not ordinary; it is a gift. It's the only day you have right now, and the only appropriate response is gratitude. If you do nothing else but cultivate that response and fully enjoy today as if it were both your first and your last, then you will have lived this day well.

Even if you feel you lack much, remember, thousands of people didn't wake up this morning, yet you are here, alive. That alone is everything.

Don't save things for "special occasions" because today is already a special occasion. If someone gives you a gift, use it. Appreciate it. When you reject a gift or keep it hidden, you send a message to yourself and the universe that you don't want, need or deserve good things. If you say "no" to life, life says "no" back to you.

Remember, the mind doesn't know the difference between imagination and reality, for the mind is the same. So why not use that to your advantage? Imagine feeling joyful, grateful and absolutely abundant. Use all your senses to appreciate what you have and to savour life, moment by moment. The more grateful you are, the happier you become. In fact, you can expand your joy simply by increasing your level of gratitude.

Gratitude and enjoyment are not passive feelings; they are active expressions of love for life.

Keep this in mind: the proof that you are living a fulfilling life is not in what you have, it's in the joy that you are manifesting from within.

Quote

❝ If you want a meaningful life, add meaning to it. Be genuine, be grateful, and treat each day as the gift it is. Don't just survive the day, live it with intention. ❞

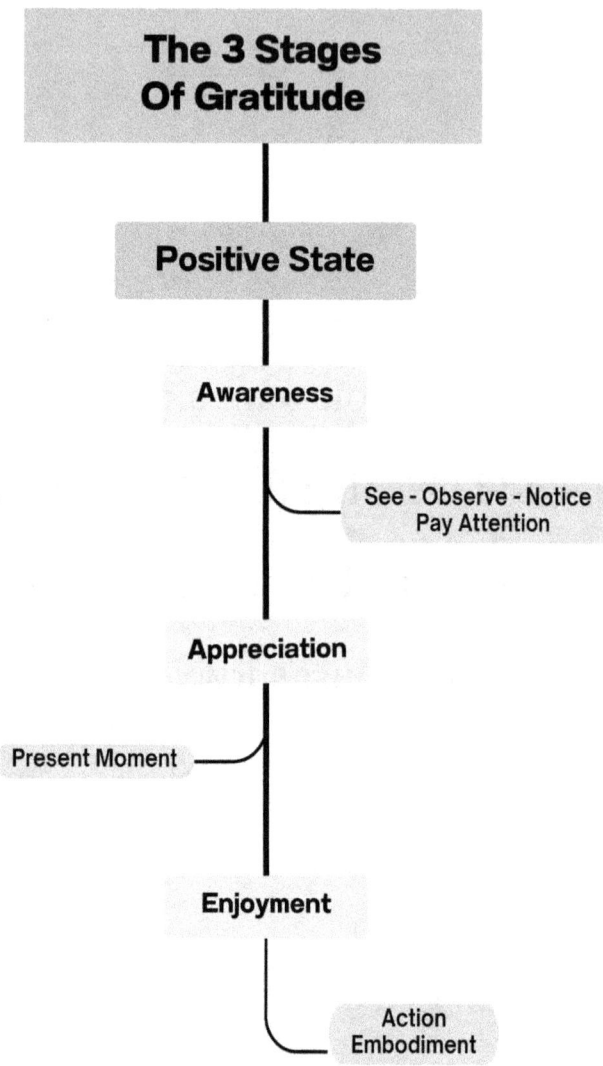

The 3 Stages of Gratitude

(Positive State)

We all move between two states: the positive and the negative.

In the positive state, gratitude unfolds in three stages: awareness, appreciation, and enjoyment.

Awareness is the first step. It begins when you notice what's already around you; when you see, observe, and pay attention to all that is present in your life.

Appreciation is the next level. It's when you take a moment to say "thank you," to feel that quiet emotion of gratitude in your heart. It's acknowledging the blessing, not just seeing it.

Then comes enjoyment, the embodiment of gratitude. This is where many people stop short. It's not enough to notice and appreciate; we must experience and engage with what we have.

For example, imagine a glass of water on your table.

- Awareness is noticing the glass — whether it's half full or half empty doesn't matter. You have water.

- Appreciation is saying, "Thank you for this water."

- Enjoyment is drinking it — savouring it, letting it refresh your body, trusting that more water will come when you need it.

If you only appreciate it but never drink it, the water will eventually become stale, dirty, and wasted. The same happens with our blessings. Gratitude that is not enjoyed becomes forgotten.

So, drink the water! Enjoy what you have now, knowing that life will always provide more.

This is where the lack mindset and the abundance mindset come into play.

When you believe there isn't enough, you hesitate, you hold back, and you "save" your joy for later, but abundance reminds you that there's always more coming, that life is generous.

Enjoyment is the highest form of gratitude. It's where joy lives. Everything around you can become an excuse to be happy, a reason to smile, to love, to be at peace.

Train yourself to find joy in the "little things", in the sound of the rain, the warmth of your tea, the laughter of a loved one. Instead of complaining about what's missing, practice being grateful for what is.

Because the truth is: happiness doesn't come from having more. It comes from fully enjoying what's already here.

"If you want a meaningful life, add meaning to it. Be genuine, be grateful, and treat each day as the gift it is. Don't just survive the day, live it with intention." - July Cortes

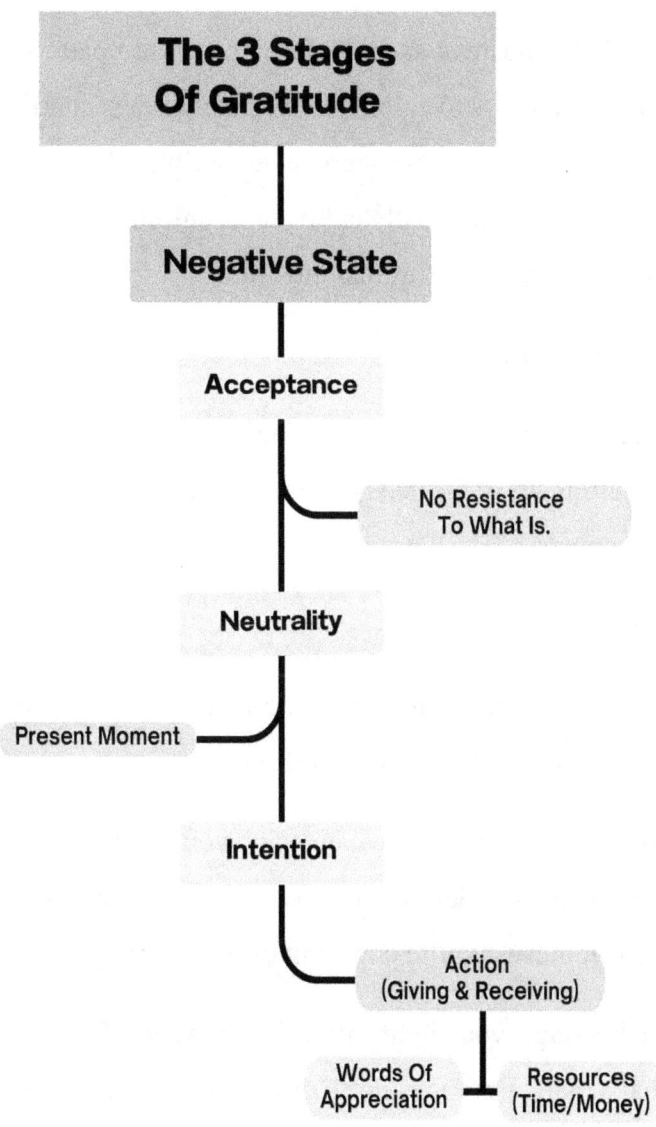

The 3 Stages of Gratitude

(Negative State)

While the positive state is a straightforward path, where we can go from awareness to enjoyment in a matter of seconds, in the negative state, gratitude doesn't come naturally; it's something we must intentionally and gently cultivate. It unfolds in three gradual stages: acceptance, neutrality, and intention.

1. Acceptance

Acceptance is the first step. It means stopping the resistance to what is, letting go of the need to control or change things that are beyond our power.

It's saying:

"This happened. I may not like it, I may not understand it, but it happened, and I cannot change that."

Maybe it's a painful breakup, a job you dislike, an accident, or a life experience that left a mark. Acceptance doesn't mean you approve of it; it means you're choosing to stop fighting against reality.

In this stage, you might still feel sadness, grief, anxiety, or anger, and that's okay. Emotions don't disappear just because you've accepted something. The goal here is not to force yourself to feel positive or grateful. If you do, you'll only create more resistance.

Remember: what you resist, persists.

Instead, allow yourself to be where you are. Feel what you feel, without judgment.

2. Neutrality

Once you've accepted what happened, you can begin moving into neutrality, a space where you're no longer consumed by the event.

Neutrality is balance. It's when you stop feeding energy to the past. You're not labelling things as "good" or "bad," "right" or "wrong." You simply say, "It is what it is, and I'm okay."

This is often the stage where people begin to rebuild — for example, after a breakup, they go back to the gym, start a new hobby, or change jobs. It's not yet happiness, it's stability. It's the quiet ground where healing starts to grow roots.

From this neutral place, you begin to make better decisions, not out of fear, anger, or desperation, but from clarity and calm.

When we make choices driven by negative emotions, those choices often lead to negative outcomes. Neutrality, on the other hand, clears the emotional fog so we can see our next steps clearly.

But neutrality is not a final destination; it's a transition. From here, we must add intention.

3. Intention

Intention is where we intentionally open ourselves to the world again. It's the conscious decision to give and to receive.

In the earlier stages of acceptance and neutrality, our energy turns inward. We're healing, protecting, and processing, but in the stage of intention, we begin to reconnect, we start to notice others again — our family, our friends, our community, the people who have supported us along the way.

Here, gratitude takes form through action. We can express it through:

- **Words of appreciation** — saying "thank you," expressing kindness and acknowledgement.

- **Resources** — giving our time, our energy, or our money.

This can look like volunteering, tithing, helping a neighbour, supporting a friend, or even inviting someone to dinner as an act that combines all three: your time, your resources, and your words of appreciation.

And as you give, something beautiful happens:

- You open the flow of energy.

- You remind yourself that you are abundant, and that what you give always comes back multiplied.

- You remind yourself that you have been loved and supported, and you are not that 'alone' as you thought.

- You are open to receiving more support, new opportunities or resources from others and life itself.

From here, you can easily and quickly move into a positive state. Gratitude will lead you into a higher frequency, where joy, peace and abundance are all available to you.

Quote

———

❝ Your standards determine the opportunities you attract. ❞

Chapter Seven

GRATITUDE X ABUNDANCE

You already hold the skills, talents, values, and strengths required to accomplish any dream. You are nature, and nature is inherently abundant, generous, and overflowing with life. Therefore, abundance isn't something outside of you; it is your true essence.

When you focus on what you don't have, you create lack, emptiness, and separation. You step out of alignment with your true nature and build an identity rooted in the belief that you are not enough as you are. You forget that the power to create and attract is always within you, ready to be accessed at any moment.

This sense of lack is not your fault; it's a conditioning we've inherited. Society has taught us that our worth depends on what we achieve, own, or prove through external validation. Only once we work hard enough, earn enough, or "deserve" enough, do we believe we can be respected and accepted, but none of that defines our value.

Your worth is innate. It comes from who you are, not from what you acquire. When you understand yourself deeply, you stop depending on outside approval and start stepping into your true power, the ability to positively influence and impact the world, no matter where you're starting from.

That's why your environment matters. Surround yourself with people who elevate your mindset, who energise and inspire you. Relationships either pull you forward or hold you back; there's no neutral. Don't be afraid to raise your standards. The wrong people will drift away, and the right ones will rise to meet you.

Your standards determine the opportunities you attract. An abundance mindset means seeing life through the lens of infinite possibilities and resources. It is not denial of reality or toxic positivity; it is meeting challenges with faith, creativity, and the belief that solutions always exist.

Abundance is also about celebrating others' successes instead of feeling threatened. It's about focusing on what you have instead of what you lack. Growth and creation are laws of nature, and whatever you wish to receive, begin by giving: love, attention, kindness, and generosity. Gratitude opens the door for this exchange, making you magnetic to opportunities, resources, and experiences.

Gratitude is the foundation of abundance. It rewires your mind, creating a fertile state for manifestation. The more grateful you are, the more abundance you perceive and receive, forming a cycle of prosperity and joy that moves you away from limitation.

Start Small

Abundance flows where your attention goes. Begin your day by recognising the gifts already present: your bed, your clothes, the food you eat, the air you breathe, the sun that warms you, and every cell in your body working tirelessly for you. Let yourself feel gratitude in your whole body, then extend it outward through words, actions, and thoughts. Gratitude multiplies when shared, creating ripples of abundance for you and others.

For example, let's say you have only a can of tuna for dinner tonight. Then make this decision: your joy is non-negotiable.

Enjoy that can of tuna as if it were made in heaven. Smile. Bless it. Feel grateful for it. Life is a mental game called Perspective, and we're all dealt two cards: Joy or Misery.

Every single moment, you get to choose which card to play.

Do I choose to feel grateful, joyful, and peaceful?
Or do I choose misery, pain, and self-pity?

I've played both cards, many times. There were days I chose the misery card: blaming, complaining, and drowning in self-pity for the life I didn't have. But that road leads nowhere. It's an endless loop of pain, poverty, and toxic energy. Nothing grows there. It only drains your spirit and keeps you stuck in agony. But when I started playing the joy card, life started responding in the most surprising ways.

Gratitude is the bridge between lack and abundance. Complaining keeps you stuck in scarcity, while appreciation places you in wealth. Take responsibility for your life; it means stop waiting, blaming, and clinging to excuses. Your past does not define your future.

Remember: what you think consistently becomes your reality.

Fear of loss creates loss; gratitude and trust create expansion. When you release what you cling to in fear, you make space for what you truly desire—love, growth, health, wealth, and joy.

Even challenges deserve your gratitude. A breakup, a rejection, or a job loss may feel painful, but they often carry hidden blessings and open doors to better opportunities. Sometimes, not getting what you want is life's greatest gift.

How I Use Gratitude As An Abundance Tool

When we talk about abundance, most people immediately think of money. And that's where the problem begins.

When we don't have enough money, when we're struggling with bills or drowning in debt, our mind automatically narrows its focus to lack. We start feeling scarcity, sadness, fear, and hopelessness. Slowly, "not having money" becomes more than a temporary situation, it becomes our identity.

But abundance, my friend, goes far beyond money. There are many forms of abundance that most people overlook:

- **Growth:** Spiritual, emotional, intellectual, and material.
- **Health:** Mental, emotional, and physical.
- **Ideas and Opportunities:** Creative flow and divine inspiration.
- **Community:** Family, friends, colleagues, neighbors, etc.
- **Enjoyment:** Play, laughter, adventure, and fun.
- **Service:** Helping others, giving without expecting anything back.
- **Basic Needs:** Food, water, shelter, clothing.
- **Nature:** Sunlight, air, water, animals, trees, and beauty all around you.

Now, you might be thinking:

"Sure, July, but you need money to have all those things!"

And I get it, I used to think the same way, especially in the days when all we had to eat was rice and eggs. It's easy to believe that money equals happiness, success, love, and well-being. But here's the truth:

The most valuable things in life, the truly priceless ones, you already have them.

Let me ask you something:

- If you woke up tomorrow without arms, how much would you pay to get them back?
- If your child didn't wake up tomorrow, how much would you give to hold them again?
- If you lost your memory or your health, how much would you pay to have them restored?

Yes, these questions are raw. Maybe even cruel. But I ask them because I want you to feel this truth deep in your heart:

Money is a wonderful tool, but it's not life itself.
It comes and goes. It can make things much easier, but it can't replace what truly matters.

You already have reasons to celebrate, to love, and to be grateful right now. Don't wait until it's too late. Don't wait to have money to feel happy, successful, or at peace. Gratitude and happiness are daily choices, not outcomes.

Never tie your peace and happiness to something you can't control, including money.

Create your Quadrants of Gratitude first, and then answer this question:

What can I create or offer with what I already possess?

Remember: money also comes in the form of ideas. Write them all down, even the "crazy" ones.

Then pick the idea that feels more aligned to you. It can be recording a video and post it on social media, or sending an email, start a tiny cleaning business, or just reaching out to a company and asking for a job. Any action that you take is better than no taking any action at all. And as you do this, make this promise to yourself. Say it with me:

"I'm not going to make my life a misery. From this moment on, no matter what happens, I only go up."

And get up. Go for it. Give your best shot, and one day, you'll look back and say: "I'm glad I did it."

Quote

❝ If you wait for the external world to give you a reason to be grateful, you remain stuck in a cycle of waiting, wishing, and hoping—reacting to life instead of creating it. ❞

Chapter Eight

GRATITUDE X MANIFESTING

The laws of the Universe teach us that gratitude is the creative force that brings manifestation into form. Everything you experience in the outer world begins in the unseen realm of thought, emotion, and belief. Nothing enters your life uninvited; you are always receiving what you are in harmony with, and that is determined by your feelings. Gratitude is one of the most powerful feelings you can embody.

Gratitude aligns you with the frequency of already having. It shifts your awareness from lack to abundance, from emptiness to fulfilment, and when you dwell in this state, the outer world rearranges itself to match your assumptions.

When you feel grateful before the evidence appears, you are declaring your blessing as already done, even if your five senses cannot yet perceive it. This isn't delusion; it's creation at its purest. What you accept as true within must express itself without. If you wait for the external world to give you a reason to be grateful, you remain stuck in a cycle of waiting, wishing, and hoping—reacting to life instead of creating it.

Gratitude breaks this passive cycle. It is not "fake it till you make it"; it is feel it because it is already yours. When you practice genuine gratitude for the abundance you hold now, you align yourself with the greater reality you desire.

One simple and funny example I can give to you is this: I love food, I really do, and I respect it also. I never waste it and I feel incredibly grateful for every meal I have, even if it's only a can of tuna and rice. Because of this, I'm excellent at manifesting food; it flows to me effortlessly.

I've come home to find a warm meal waiting for me, left by a colleague. I've been given free pizza or drinks in restaurants for no reason at all. Friends cook for me without me asking. Once, I even manifested five boxes of pizza!

It's crazy how it happened. It was around 3 p.m., and as I walked past a pizza shop, I thought, "I'd love to eat pizza tonight." Later, I told my flatmate, "We should go out for pizza tonight, what about 9 p.m?" She agreed. Time passed, and we both got busy. At exactly 9 p.m., someone knocked on the door. I opened it, and there stood a delivery guy with boxes of pizza, five of them!

I assumed my flatmate had ordered, but she hadn't. We called the shop, but no one answered. So we laughed, blessed the mystery, and had pizza for almost a week, and I freaking loved it.

That's how life works when you live in gratitude and actually enjoy what you have. Life keeps giving you more things to be grateful for, in the most unexpected ways.

When your heart is open, when your energy is joyful, life matches that frequency.

Gratitude, in this sense, becomes a spiritual declaration. Belief is not a thought; it is a felt knowing, and gratitude is the emotional expression of that belief.

To thank the Universe or God in advance is the highest form of prayer; you are not begging or pleading in desperation, but you are claiming.

You are stepping into the secret chamber of your own consciousness and assuming the feeling of the wish fulfilled. Gratitude is not for what has happened outside, but for what is already true in the unseen.

This practice seals your assumptions. It breaks the old pattern of "needing proof before believing" and frees you from appearances. From this higher state, the world becomes responsive: opportunities unfold, connections appear, conditions shift, and all is reflecting the vibration of gratitude you are holding.

Your consistent feelings of gratitude become the blueprint of your future. It is the conscious choice to dwell in the end and embody your outcome now.

The Universe doesn't respond to occasional positive words or gestures. Gratitude is the mark of assumption, attraction, and faith. It is the vibration of "I have already received", and once you feel it, the necessary means of physical manifestation are set into motion.

To be truly grateful is to trust the unseen, to dare to believe that consciousness creates reality. Gratitude arises naturally when you are no longer waiting; you are living from the end. Even in hard times, gratitude becomes your weapon of higher vibration; saying "thank you" in the face of adversity is the sign of true spirituality. Gratitude is the flame within that precedes the outer light.

Gratitude changes you. It shifts your posture, your thoughts, and your energy. It silences doubt, dissolves resistance, and places you in harmony with creation. When you feel grateful, you're not asking for something; you're declaring its presence. You collapse the gap between yourself and what you desire. You stop looking for it, because you already feel whole.

Everything operates on frequency, and gratitude is the clearest signal of manifestation; it broadcasts the energy of fulfilment, not longing. In true gratitude, there is no tension, no doubt—only peace, certainty, and alignment.

And when you hold this vibration:

- People respond differently.

- New opportunities arrive.

- The world reorganises itself around your state.

Whether it's love, abundance, health, or success—the process is always the same:

- Feel it first.

- Embody gratitude.

- Act from it.

Let gratitude be your evidence. The feeling comes before the fact, not after.

When you consistently practice this state, you stop postponing happiness and start creating your future now. Gratitude silences fear and anchors you in inspired action. Life begins to flow because you have shifted, not because circumstances changed first, but because you changed.

Gratitude is not just a practice—it is your companion, your evidence, your alignment with who you are meant to be.

Practice: Active Faith ("Act As If")

Active faith means believing first and preparing yourself as if what you desire is already yours. Visualise it, feel it, speak of it, act in alignment with it. The subconscious loves repetition and preparation, and when you live consistently from the end, your success becomes inevitable.

On the other hand, fear is faith misdirected. If you dwell on what you don't want—talking about it, imagining it, and repeating it, you are magnetising it into form just as powerfully. The law works either way.

Exercise: Live From The End

Create a "miniature version" of your ideal reality.

- Want to be generous? Give $1 or one hour of your time to charity.

- Want wealth? Save or invest $10 a week.

- Want deeper love? Dedicate an hour daily to your loved ones.

- Want health? Move your body 10 minutes a day.

If you can't practice the habits of your dream life now, you won't do them later when you "arrive." Small actions create alignment. They build the discipline and identity that call your reality into being.

Live from the end. Give thanks as if it's already yours. Get the inside right and the outside will take care of itself.

About The Author

July Cortes is an entrepreneur, Certified Spiritual Hypnosis Practitioner, and Gratitude 4 Manifesting teacher originally from Colombia, but living in New Zealand.

Her purpose is simple yet profound:
"To serve all who want to manifest joy, love, and abundance from within."

Before living her purpose, July walked a long and challenging path. Coming from a very poor family and facing extreme poverty with few opportunities, she worked tirelessly to rise above her circumstances and rebuild herself from the ground up. Her journey is a living example that transformation is possible, and no matter where you begin, you can create a life filled with meaning, joy, and abundance.

Today, July is on a mission to make gratitude go viral — to share the tools, wisdom, and mindset that helped her transform her own life, so others can do the same. Through her teachings, she helps people reconnect with themselves, heal from within, and manifest their highest potential.

When she's not working or studying, you'll find July enjoying a good cup of coffee, eating bananas, recharging her energy at the gym, or chilling in nature.

www.ingramcontent.com/pod-product-compliance
Lightning Source LLC
LaVergne TN
LVHW021614080426
835510LV00019B/2562